W9-AJT-311

Arthropods

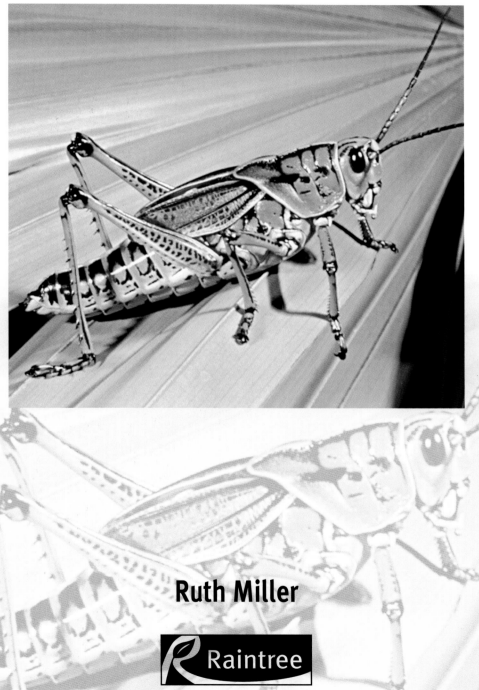

Ruth Miller

Raintree

Chicago, Illinois

For information, address the publisher:
Raintree, 100 N. LaSalle, Suite 1200, Chicago, IL 60602

Produced for Raintree by
White-Thomson Publishing Ltd.

Consultant: Dr. Rod Preston-Mafham
Page layout by Tim Mayer
Photo research by Morgan Interactive Ltd.

Originated by Dot Gradations Ltd.
Printed in China by WKT Company Limited

09 08 07 06 05
10 9 8 7 6 5 4 3 2 1

Library of Congress Cataloging-in-Publication Data
Miller, Ruth, 1936-
    Arthropods / Ruth Miller.
        p. cm. -- (Animal kingdom)
    Includes bibliographical references (p.   ).
    ISBN 1-4109-1049-0 (lib. bdg.-hardcover) -- ISBN 1-4109-
1343-0 (pbk.)
    1. Arthropoda--Juvenile literature. [1. Arthropods.] I. Title.
II.Series: Animal kingdom (Chicago, Ill.)
    QL434.15.M67 2004
    595--dc22

                            2003026831

Acknowledgments
The publisher would like to thank the following for permission to
reproduce copyright materials: Corbis p.35 top; Digital Vision
Title page, pp. 4, 6, 8, 18 bottom, 19, 24 top, 28 top, 29 top,
48 bottom, 53 bottom, 58, 60, 61; Ecoscene pp. 11 top (Chinch
Gryniewicz), 15 top (Wayne Lawler), 17 top (Fritz Pölking), 21
top, 24 bottom (Kjell Sandved), 27 bottom (Robin Williams),
29 (Chinch Gryniewicz), 33 top (Jeff Collett), 50-51 (Martin
Lillicrap), 55 top (Erik Schaffer), 55 bottom (Chinch
Gryniewicz), 56 (Tom Ennis), 57 top (Chinch Gryniewicz);
Ecoscene-Papilio pp. 10 (Lando Pescatori), 11 bottom (William
Dunn), 12 top (Lando Pescatori), 14 and 16 (Robert Pickett),
18 top (Alastair Shay), 22 (Lando Pescatori), 23 top, 31 top
(Robert Pickett), 40, 41 top, 42 bottom, 54 (Robert Pickett);
Nature PL pp. 34, 35 bottom (Jurgen Freund), 36 (Chris
Packham), 48 top (Bernard Castelein), 53 top (John Cancalosi);
NHPA pp. 5 top (Daniel Heuclin), 7 top (James Carmichael), 9
top, 13 (Stephen Dalton), 15 bottom (Nigel Callow), 16-17
(Stephen Dalton), 21 bottom (Anthony Bannister), 23 bottom
(Pete Oxford), 25 (Stephen Dalton), 26 (Eric Solder), 27 top
(John Shaw), 31 bottom (Nigel Callow), 32 top (Yves Lanceau),
37 top (B Jones and M Shimlock), 37 bottom (Anthony
Bannister), 38 (G.I. Bernard), 39 top (Anthony Bannister), 41
bottom (B Jones and M Shimlock), 43 top, 45 bottom (Daniel
Heuclin), 46 top (Peter Parks), 46 bottom (Anthony Bannister),
47 (Daniel Heuclin), 49 top (Stephen Dalton), 50 left (ANT), 51
right (James Carmichael), 52 (Daniel Heuclin), 57 bottom
(Stephen Dalton); Photodisc Contents page, 5 bottom, 7 bottom,
9 bottom, 30, 33 bottom, 44, 45 top, 59; Premaphotos Wildlife
pp. 20, 39, 43 bottom (Preston-Mafham).

Front cover photograph of Sally Lightfoot crabs reproduced with
permission of Corbis (Martin Harvey/Gallo Images). Back cover
photograph of a honey bee reproduced with permission of
Digital Vision.

Every effort has been made to contact copyright holders of any
material reproduced in this book. Any omissions will be rectified
in subsequent printings if notice is given to the publishers.

Contents

INTRODUCING ARTHROPODS 4

ARTHROPOD FEATURES 6

INSECTS 8

Insect Life Cycles 10

Insect Flight 12

Butterflies and Moths 14

The Monarch Butterfly 16

Ants, Bees, and Wasps 18

Termites 20

Bugs 22

Beetles 24

Dragonflies and Damselflies 26

Flies 28

CRUSTACEA 30

Crabs and Lobsters 32

Prawns and Shrimp 36

Copepods and Barnacles 38

Minor Classes 40

CENTIPEDES AND MILLIPEDES 42

ARACHNIDS 44

Spiders 48

Orb Web Spiders 50

Scorpions 52

ARTHROPODS UNDER THREAT 54

Protecting Arthropods 56

CLASSIFICATION 58

Arthropod Evolution 60

GLOSSARY 62

FURTHER INFORMATION 63

INDEX 64

Introducing Arthropods

Arthropods are invertebrates. This means they do not have internal bony skeletons and they do not have backbones. Three out of four of all known animal species are arthropods. More than a million species of living and fossil arthropods have been described and named. They are found in all climates and a wide range of habitats—from oceans to high mountains.

Chewers and nonchewers

Most scientists divide the phylum Arthropoda into two major groups or subphyla—Mandibulata and Chelicerata—depending on the shape of their mouthparts and whether or not they have sensory feelers called antennae.

Arthropods with chewing mouthparts called mandibles and one or two pairs of antennae are classified as mandibulates. This large group includes hexapods (insects and other six-legged arthropods), myriapods (centipedes and millipedes), and crustaceans (water fleas, crabs, and lobsters). Some scientists think that the mandibulates should be further divided into two groups—crustaceans and uniramians—to separate crabs and lobsters from insects and myriapods.

Chelicerates have pincerlike appendages on the head and do not have antennae. This group includes arachnids (spiders, mites, and ticks), sea spiders, and horseshoe crabs.

▼ Ants are arthropods with well-developed mandibles. These social insects are found all over the world and live in highly organized colonies.

Classification key

KINGDOM	Animalia
PHYLUM	**Arthropoda**
SUBPHYLA	Mandibulata and Chelicerata
CLASSES	9–6 Mandibulata and 3 Chelicerata
ORDERS	99
FAMILIES	about 2,140
SPECIES	over 1,077,500

▲ Most fiddler crab
species live in the mud
of mangrove swamps
in tropical climates.
They have eyes on long
stalks. Males have one
enormous claw, which
they wave to attract
females and warn off
rival males.

Classification

Living organisms are classified, or organized, according
to how closely related one organism is to another. The
basic group in classification is the species. For example,
human beings belong to the species *Homo sapiens*. A
species is a group of individuals that are similar to each
other and that can interbreed with one another. Species
are grouped together into genera (singular: genus). A
genus may contain a number of species that share some
features. *Homo* is the human genus. Genera are grouped
together in families, families are grouped into orders,
and orders are grouped into classes. Classes are
grouped together in phyla (singular: phylum), and,
finally, the phyla are grouped into kingdoms.
Kingdoms are the largest groups. Arthropods belong
to the animal kingdom.

◀ Tarantulas are the
largest spiders. Their
bodies may grow to
a width of 4.8 inches
(12 centimeters)
and they may have
a leg span of up to
11.2 inches
(28 centimeters).

Arthropod Features

Arthropods have segmented bodies with jointed legs. The body is covered on the outside with a tough, flexible layer called the cuticle. This layer forms an outer skeleton, or exoskeleton. Other animals, such as mammals and birds, have a bony skeleton inside the body that is called an endoskeleton. In most groups of arthropods, the body has three distinct parts: the head, the thorax, and the abdomen. The bodies of most arthropods are clearly divided into a number of segments, or compartments. The head contains the brain. The head is made up of six segments, but the segments are not clearly defined as in the thorax and the abdomen. The head has paired mouthparts for feeding and sense organs such as eyes.

Jointed legs

The most characteristic feature of the arthropods is their appendages, the jointed structures attached to the body segments. The appendages on an arthropod's head are adapted to help in feeding, while those on the rest of the body, which are usually adapted for walking or swimming, are often referred to as legs. In some arthropods, appendages on the abdomen may be adapted for reproduction.

▼ Scorpions show characteristic arthropod features. They are easily recognized by their large, clawlike pedipalps and their curved tails.

▼ Wood borers are beetles that live in dead wood. Their mouthparts are adapted for making tunnels through the lumber.

Exoskeleton

An important feature of arthropods is the hard, rigid exoskeleton. It provides support for locomotion and protection from enemies. The exoskeleton also prevents the body organs from being damaged or from losing too much water. This type of skeleton has to be shed to allow for the animal's growth. All arthropods undergo molting, or shedding, of the cuticle. While the new exoskeleton is hardening, the animal can increase in size.

Respiration

In most land arthropods, such as insects, gas exchange for respiration takes place through a system of air-filled tubes called tracheae. Trachea transport air directly to the body tissues. They open to the outside of the body through a series of tiny pores, or spiracles, in the cuticle. Most water arthropods, such as crabs and lobsters, breathe using gills.

▼ The phylum Arthropoda includes a wide range of very different-looking animals. However, there are some shared characteristics.

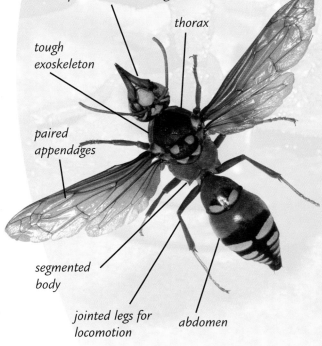

The head is distinct, with paired mouthparts and sense organs.

thorax

tough exoskeleton

paired appendages

segmented body

jointed legs for locomotion

abdomen

Amazing facts

- The phylum Arthropoda gets its name from the Greek word *arthros,* which means "joint" and *podos,* which means "foot."
- Some arthropods, such as crustaceans, tarantulas, and funnel-web spiders, molt throughout their lives. However, among insects usually just the larvae molt.
- During molting, an arthropod is vulnerable to attacks by predators because its body is soft and unprotected.

Insects

Insects first appeared about 300 to 550 million years ago and are thought to have evolved from myriapod-like ancestors. Many species of insects live on land, but large numbers are found in freshwater habitats such as lakes, rivers, and ponds. Most insects are small, and their tough exoskeletons prevent them from losing water. This means they can survive in dry conditions. Insects with wings can travel long distances in search of food, mates, and suitable places to live. This means they are found in a wide range of habitats.

An insect's body is made up of three parts—the head, the thorax, and the abdomen. On the head are mouthparts, a pair of compound eyes, and one pair of antennae. The main characteristics of insects that separate them from other arthropods are their three pairs of jointed legs and one or two pairs of wings attached to the thorax. The abdomen is segmented and does not have any appendages.

Sense organs

Insects have well-developed sense organs. Insect antennae are sensitive to touch and to chemicals in the environment. Insects use their antennae for information about food sources, mates, and other members of their own species. The large compound eyes are made up of many thousands of tiny structures, called ommatidia, each with its own lens. Each lens points in a slightly different direction, and each forms an image. The images formed are not sharply defined, but the insect can detect movements and shapes. An insect has other sense organs in the cuticle and on the limbs that respond to touch and chemicals.

Classification key

PHYLUM	Arthropoda
SUBPHYLUM	Mandibulata
SUPERCLASS	Hexapoda
CLASS	**Insecta**
ORDERS	29
FAMILIES	949
SPECIES	over 1 million

▼ Grasshoppers show many common insect features. The large compound eyes and sensitive antennae can be seen here.

Noninsect hexapods

Having three pairs of legs places insects in the superclass Hexapoda, with collembolans, proturans and diplurans. These three groups, which are known as noninsect hexapods, are found all over the world. The collembolans, such as *Sminthus viridis,* and the proturans, such as *Eosentomon delicatum,* are 0.8 inches (2 millimeters) long and live in soil and leaf litter. The diplurans, such as the common North American species *Catajapyx diversiunguis,* are larger. None of these groups has wings, and many lack eyes and antennae. Their mouthparts are in a pouch underneath the head.

Classification key

PHYLUM	Arthropoda
SUBPHYLUM	Mandibulata
SUPERCLASS	Hexapoda
CLASS	**Collembola**
FAMILIES	18
SPECIES	6500
CLASS	**Protura**
FAMILIES	4
SPECIES	400
CLASS	**Diplura**
FAMILIES	9
SPECIES	800

Amazing facts

- Insects were the first creatures to live on land. They appeared about 200 million years before the dinosaurs.
- The world's longest insect is the giant stick insect of Indonesia, which grows to a length of about 12 inches (30 centimeters).

Segmented antennae covered with tiny hairs. These are sensitive to smell, touch, and temperature.

The large compound eyes give an all-around view.

Three pairs of jointed legs. While walking, the insect has three legs in contact with the ground and three legs moving forward.

Two pairs of wings. The front wings are thicker than the hind wings, which are thin like membranes.

Segmented abdomen with spiracles. Adult insects breathe air, which enters through openings called spiracles that are located on the sides of the abdomen and thorax.

▲ All insects share some common features. This is a flower mantid.

Insect Life Cycles

Insects lay eggs that hatch into larvae. The larvae feed, grow rapidly, and undergo several molts before they become adults and are able to breed. The change from larva to adult is called metamorphosis.

▶ Caterpillars, such as this vaporer moth caterpillar, are larvae that begin eating as soon as they hatch. They grow rapidly and molt several times.

Metamorphosis

In some insects, such as locusts, the eggs hatch into larvae called nymphs. Locust nymphs look similar to the adults, but they do not have wings. Instead, there are little pads where the wings will develop later. As the larvae grow, they molt. After the final molt, the mature insect emerges, complete with wings. This type of metamorphosis, which is made up of three life cycle stages, is called incomplete metamorphosis.

Other insects, such as butterflies and beetles, have four distinct life cycle stages—egg, larva, pupa, and adult. This type of metamorphosis is called complete metamorphosis. The eggs hatch into larvae that are called grubs, maggots, or caterpillars, depending on the species. The larvae feed and molt several times, growing rapidly until they reach their full size. They then enter the pupal stage, where all the larval body parts break down and the adult parts are formed. During this stage, the insect is inactive and does not feed. In many insects, the pupal stage takes place inside a protective case called a cocoon or chrysalis. When the adult emerges from the pupa, it is fully mature and able to breed.

◀ When the ladybug larva is fully grown, it molts and the new skin hardens to form a pupal case. Inside this case, the pupa develops into the adult.

Larvae

Larvae represent the feeding and growing stages in the insect life cycle. Their way of life, food, method of locomotion, and habitat are usually very different from those of the adults of the same species. In some species, such as caddis flies, the larvae are aquatic, whereas the adults live on land and can fly. The length of time it takes to complete the life cycle varies from one species to another and can also depend on the time of year. Aquatic larvae, such as mayfly larvae, may take a year or more to develop into adults. The adults survive for only a few hours—long enough to mate and lay eggs.

Amazing facts

- Female butterflies stamp on the leaves of a plant to test whether they are ripe enough to lay eggs on.
- Periodical cicadas of North America may take between thirteen and seventeen years to become adults and be able to breed.
- In dragonflies, the larval stage may last several years. The nymphs are aquatic and feed on tadpoles and young fish.

▲ Just before an adult dragonfly emerges, the chrysalis becomes darker. The adult's wings are crumpled at first. The dragonfly pumps blood into the veins of its wings to straighten them out.

Insect Flight

Insects are the only invertebrates that can fly. Winged insects can travel long distances in search of food, mates, and new habitats. They can escape from their enemies and quickly move to more favorable conditions. These factors have contributed to their success as a group.

Wings

Insects' wings are flattened extensions of the cuticle. A network of veins strengthens and supports them. Most winged insects have two pairs of wings attached to the thorax.

▲ The hardened front wings of beetles, such as the ladybug, are called elytra. They protect the delicate hind wings when the beetle is not flying.

The base of each wing lies between the plates, or sclerites, that form the top and sides of the exoskeleton. In flight, the wing moves like a see-saw. Its position allows a small amount of muscle movement to cause a large movement of the wing.

In some insects, such as dragonflies and butterflies, the two pairs of wings are similar. In other groups, such as beetles and cockroaches, the front wings are hard or leathery. They protect the thinner, membranelike hind wings. True flies (Diptera) have front wings that are thin and membranelike, but their hind wings have adapted to form a pair of small, club-shaped structures called halteres. These act as balancing organs, helping the fly to keep on its course and make rapid changes in direction.

Amazing facts

- The buzzing of a fly is the sound of its wings beating. The wings of midges beat about 1,000 times a second.
- Butterflies may bask in the sun to warm up their wing muscles before flying. The wings absorb energy like solar panels.

Flight muscles

A dragonfly has flight muscles attached to the bases of its wings and thorax. When the muscles attached to the wings contract, the wings are pushed downward. This is called a downstroke. An upstroke occurs when the muscles attached to the thorax contract. Beetles and butterflies do not have flight muscles directly attached to the wings. Instead, wing movements are brought about by muscle contraction, which changes the shape of the thorax.

Many insects need to beat their wings very rapidly in order to stay in the air. This type of flight requires a great deal of energy. Butterflies and moths fly in a different way. They flap their wings slowly up and down, like birds, and can use air currents to stay in the air.

▶ True flies, such as this dronefly, have a single pair of thin, membranelike front wings.

▲ Adult locusts gather together in large groups called swarms and fly to new feeding grounds.

13

Butterflies and Moths

Butterflies and moths are found worldwide, with the exception of Antarctica. They all have two pairs of wings covered in tiny scales and undergo complete metamorphosis during their life cycles. In general, butterflies are brightly colored, have clubbed antennae, and are active during the day. Their bodies are thin and relatively hairless, and they settle with their wings folded so that the undersides are exposed. Moths usually have fatter, hairy bodies, and their antennae are often feathery but never clubbed. Moths fly at dusk or during the night. When they settle, their wings are spread flat with the upper surface showing. Many moths have dull colors, but several have brightly colored wings and spectacular markings.

Feeding

Adult butterflies and moths feed on nectar and other liquids through a long sucking tube called a proboscis that is coiled under the head when not in use. Caterpillars, or butterfly larvae, have biting mouthparts called mandibles that they use to chew plant material. Adults do not have mandibles. Caterpillars feed all the time, and their numerous legs give them a firm hold on their food. Caterpillars have three pairs of true legs on the thorax and five pairs of fleshy prolegs (legs without joints) on the abdomen.

▼ The amazing colors of the Asian comet moth's wings are due to its covering of scales. Each scale is a tiny flattened hair that is either colored or reflects the light in a certain way.

Classification key

PHYLUM	Arthropoda
SUBPHYLUM	Mandibulata
SUPERCLASS	Hexapoda
CLASS	Insecta
ORDER	**Lepidoptera**
FAMILIES	127
SPECIES	about 165,000

▲ This brightly colored moth caterpillar is covered in tiny bristles to ward off predators.

Mating

Adult butterflies and moths live long enough only to mate and lay their eggs. Males and females produce chemical substances called pheromones that attract the opposite sex. Females have scent glands on the abdomen and the males produce pheromones from special scales on the wings. A female mates once and then produces a pheromone that prevents other males from mating with her. Males mate several times.

Skippers

Skippers are different from most butterflies and share some characteristics with moths. They have hooked, not clubbed, antennae and plump, hairy bodies. They get their name from their darting flight, their rapid wing beats, and their ability to suddenly change direction. Like many moths, skipper pupae are encased in a cocoon.

Amazing facts

- Queen Alexandra's birdwing butterfly, which is found only in New Guinea, is the world's largest butterfly. Females may have a wingspan of up to 11.2 inches (28 centimeters).

- The smallest butterfly in the world, the pygmy blue, has a wingspan of between 0.44 and 0.72 inches (11 and 18 millimeters).

- The caterpillars of the orchard swallowtail butterfly are camouflaged to look like bird droppings. This adaptation helps them hide from their enemies.

▶ A butterfly's proboscis unfurls like a straw to suck up nectar. An increase in the butterfly's blood pressure causes the proboscis to extend.

The Monarch Butterfly

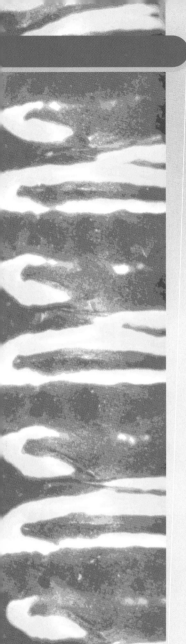

The monarch butterfly is most common in North, Central, and South America. Adult American monarchs have bright orange wings with black veins and outer margins and a wingspan of about 4 inches (10 centimeters). Their bodies are black with white spots. Both larvae and adults feed on a plant called milkweed, which contains chemicals that are poisonous to their predators. The adults feed on the nectar in the flowers and the larvae eat the leaves.

Life cycle

The female butterfly lays her eggs on the undersides of milkweed leaves. The eggs take about three to fifteen days to hatch. The caterpillar eats its way out of the egg and then begins to feed on the milkweed leaves. It continues to feed for the next fifteen days. During that period the caterpillar will molt four times.

When it has reached about two inches (five centimeters) long, the caterpillar stops feeding, finds a branch, and attaches itself by means of a silk pad. It molts one last time and its skin then hardens to form the pupa, or chrysalis. Inside the pupa, the larval body parts break down and the adult ones are formed. This stage takes about ten to twelve days. Finally, the chrysalis splits down the back and the adult butterfly emerges.

Adult monarch butterflies are ready to mate about three to eight days after emerging from the chrysalis. They may mate several times during their lives. The females begin to lay their eggs immediately after mating.

▼ Milkweed plants contain a poisonous substance that is absorbed by the bodies of monarch caterpillars. The poison protects them from being eaten by vertebrate predators such as birds and mice.

Classification key

PHYLUM	Arthropoda
SUBPHYLUM	Mandibulata
SUPERCLASS	Hexapoda
CLASS	Insecta
ORDER	Lepidoptera
FAMILIES	Danaidae
GENUS	*Danaus*
SPECIES	***Danaus plexippus***

Amazing facts

- Large colonies of migrating butterflies are found in Mexico. Between 15,000 and 20,000 monarch butterflies may roost on one tree branch.

- In order to follow the migration, scientists have glued tiny paper tags onto the wings of the butterflies. One butterfly tagged in Minnesota flew to Mexico, a distance of 1,844 miles (3,122 kilometers).

▶ Monarch butterflies feed on nectar. They visit a range of different flowers including milkweed, clover, and thistles.

Migration

In the northern United States and in southern Canada, the monarchs breed during the summer. In autumn, as the weather gets colder, most of the adult butterflies migrate to the southern United States and Mexico. They spend the winter there, often gathering in large numbers. In the spring, the butterflies start returning north. During this migration, they mate and produce offspring. Several generations of butterflies will be born during the migration north. Therefore, a different generation of butterflies returns to the north than the one that left. The life span of the adult butterflies that emerge in the autumn is about eight months. However, the adult butterflies produced in spring and summer months during the return migration live only for about four to six weeks.

▶ Hibernating butterflies form dense clusters on trees. Each hangs with its wings down over the one below it. This provides protection from rain and helps to keep the group warm.

17

Ants, Bees, and Wasps

The insects in the order Hymenoptera have two pairs of delicate, membranous wings, with the front pair larger than the hind pair. The wings are coupled together with a row of hooks on the front edge of the hind wings.

▶ Bees collect nectar and pollen from flowers. As the bees visit the flowers, they transfer pollen from one plant to another and bring about pollination.

Characteristic features

Ants, bees, wasps, and ichneumon flies belong to the suborder Apocrita. They have a narrow kind of waist between the thorax and the abdomen. The mouthparts are adapted for biting, but they can also sip liquids, such as nectar. The larvae are legless with small heads. Female bees, wasps, and some ants have stingers at the tips of the abdomen.

Sawflies belong to the suborder Symphyta. They do not have a narrow waist between the thorax and the abdomen. They do not sting, and their larvae are similar to caterpillars, with definite heads, legs, and prolegs. Sawflies show no social behavior, and none are parasites.

▲ Two pairs of delicate wings and a definite waist between the thorax and the abdomen are characteristic of wasps and bees. The bees shown above are storing collected nectar in the cells of a honeycomb.

Social insects

Many ants, bees, and wasps live in large groups, or colonies. In colonies, all the individuals belong to the same family and are often the offspring of a single female. They are known as social insects. There are usually several different types of individuals, or castes, in one colony, all performing different jobs. In a honeybee colony, for example, there is one egg-laying female, called the queen; several thousand sterile females called worker bees; and a few hundred male bees, or drones. Males develop from unfertilized eggs. Their function is to mate with the queen. Drones are fed by the workers from stores of nectar and pollen. They live for only a few weeks. Fertilized eggs hatch into larvae, which may develop into workers or queens depending on the food they are given. Larvae that are to become queens are fed on royal jelly, a rich substance that comes from the workers, until they pupate. Larvae that will develop into workers are given diluted nectar and pollen after three days. The workers collect nectar and pollen, look after the larvae, clean the hive, and feed the queen.

Amazing facts

- Wasps do not make honey. They feed on nectar, fruit juices, or smaller creatures.
- The stinger of a honeybee is barbed. It cannot be withdrawn from human skin without leaving behind the barb and venom sac. This damages the abdomen of the bee and kills it.

Classification key

PHYLUM	Arthropoda
SUBPHYLUM	Mandibulata
SUPERCLASS	Hexapoda
CLASS	Insecta
ORDER	Hymenoptera
SUBORDER	**Symphyta (sawflies) Apocrita (ants, bees, and wasps)**
FAMILIES	91
SPECIES	at least 198,000

▼ Leaf cutter ants feed on fungus that they grow in their underground nests. They grow the fungus on pieces of leaves they collect and take back to the nest.

Termites

Most termite species live in the tropics, but a few are found in southern Europe and in the United States. Termites resemble true ants and are often confused with them. However, true ants have a kind of waist between their thoraxes and abdomens, while termites do not. True ants are related to bees and wasps, but termites are more closely related to cockroaches.

Castes

Termite colonies contain four types of castes. There is usually one fertile, egg-laying queen and a male king who fertilizes the eggs. There are also large numbers of small, white, sterile, wingless males and females called workers. The workers build the nest, find food, groom other members of the colony, and guard the eggs. In addition, there are soldier that are also sterile and wingless. The soldiers have enlarged heads bearing huge jaws or long snouts. Soldiers guard the colony and protect the workers as they collect food.

Classification key

PHYLUM	Arthropoda
SUBPHYLUM	Mandibulata
SUPERCLASS	Hexapoda
CLASS	Insecta
ORDER	Isoptera
FAMILY	**Termitidae**
SPECIES	1,950

▶ Termite mounds are constructed of soil cemented with saliva and baked in the sun. Inside there are many chambers connected by passages and ducts to allow air to circulate.

Forming new colonies

At certain times, winged male and female termites develop in the colonies. These have harder, darker bodies and compound eyes. When they are mature, the winged termites fly off in swarms and pair up to start new colonies. After their flight, they shed their wings and mate. The female lays eggs and becomes queen of the new colony. Her abdomen becomes swollen with thousands of eggs. In some species, the queen termite grows many times larger than a normal female. The eggs hatch into nymphs that look like the adults. They go through an incomplete metamorphosis, becoming more like the adults after each molt.

▲ The queen becomes as long as 4 inches (10 centimeters) in some species.

The king and queen produce chemical substances that prevent workers from producing offspring that would compete for food and living space. Workers lick these substances off the bodies of the king and queen and pass them on to other members of the colony during grooming. When the queen dies, these substances run out, causing some nymphs to develop reproductive organs so that they can produce offspring.

▲ The soldier termites guard and protect the worker termites while they gather food for the colony.

Amazing facts

- In west Africa, people eat fat, juicy termite queens. In some countries, insects are considered tasty and nutritious additions to the diet.

- In some termite species, the queen termite becomes very large and may lay 30,000 eggs in one day.

- A colony can contain several hundred to several million termites.

Bugs

Bugs form a large order of insects called Hemiptera. They are found all over the world. They vary in size from tiny whiteflies, which are about 0.12 inches (3 millimeters) long, to large cicadas, which have wingspans of up to 6 inches (15 centimeters). All bugs have two pairs of wings and slender, needle-like mouthparts for piercing and sucking their food. Their eggs hatch into nymphs that feed on the same kind of food as the adults. Adults and nymphs are often found together. Nymphs grow into adults by incomplete metamorphosis.

Bugs or beetles?

Many bugs, such as shield bugs or stink bugs, look like beetles. However, their mouthparts and front wings are different. All beetles have biting mouthparts. The front wings of a beetle meet in the middle. The entire front wing is hard and forms a protective covering for the hind wings. The ends of the front wings of a bug overlap, and the tips of these wings are membranous.

▼ To attract females or ward off enemies, male cicadas make shrill noises by rapidly vibrating two small membranes on either side of the abdomen.

Amazing facts

- All species of the genus of pond skaters *Halobates* are marine and live on the surface of tropical and subtropical seas. They lay their eggs on floating seaweed.
- The red food dye cochineal is extracted from a species of scale insect, the cochineal bug. It was first used by the Aztecs in Mexico hundreds of years ago.
- Some male cicadas produce calls that can be heard almost 1 mile (1.5 kilometers) away.

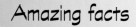

▲ Pond skaters have long middle and hind legs that are spread out to support their weight on the surface of the water. They move across the surface using the rowing action of their middle legs.

Classification key

PHYLUM	Arthropoda
SUBPHYLUM	Mandibulata
SUPERCLASS	Hexapoda
CLASS	Insecta
ORDER	**Hemiptera**
FAMILIES	134
SPECIES	82,000

Wings and mouthparts

This order of insects can be divided into two groups that are based on differences in wing structure and in the position of the beaklike mouthparts called the rostrum. In the group Heteroptera, which contains the shield bugs, the front wings are divided into two parts. The part that is attached to the body is tough and leathery, while the tip is delicate and membranous. The rostrum is at the front of the head. This group includes capsid bugs, bedbugs, and aquatic species such as pond skaters.

Cicadas, leafhoppers, and aphids belong to the group Homoptera. In this group the rostrum comes from the back part of the head and the front wings are not divided. These insects are either completely stiffened or completely membranous. Cicadas and leafhoppers have short, bristle-like antennae, but aphids, whiteflies, and male scale insects have long, threadlike antennae. Female scale insects do not have legs, wings, or antennae. They have bodies covered by a hard scale which gives the group its name. The males have wings but lack scales, and they look like tiny midges.

▲ Shield bugs get their name from their flattened shape, which looks like a shield.

23

Beetles

There are more known beetle species in the world than any other insect. Beetles are found in a wide range of habitats on land and in water. This group includes ladybugs, dung beetles, and the aquatic whirligig beetles. Their success is due to the tough cuticle that covers their bodies. They all have hard front wings, called elytra, which protect their delicate membranous hind wings. Beetles can live under stones, in leaf litter, and in water. They are not easily damaged, and they can survive in dry places because the tough cuticle prevents their bodies from losing water. All beetles have biting jaws used for feeding. In some species, the jaws have been adapted for fighting. There is also some variation in the structure of the legs, which may be used for walking, swimming, or digging.

▲ The bright colors of this beetle's front wings signal to predators that it has a nasty taste.

Classification key

PHYLUM	Arthropoda
SUBPHYLUM	Mandibulata
SUPERCLASS	Hexapoda
CLASS	Insecta
ORDER	**Coleoptera**
FAMILIES	166
SPECIES	370,000

▲ Weevils are sometimes called snout beetles. The head has a beak-shaped structure, called a rostrum, with a pair of mandibles, or jaws, at the tip.

Beetle life cycle

The beetle life cycle involves a complete metamorphosis. Beetles may lay their eggs near a food source for the larvae, but some just scatter the eggs. The larvae, usually called grubs, do not look like their parents. They look like worms but have well-developed heads with biting jaws similar to those of adults. Adults and larvae are often found on the same food source. The larvae feed and grow, molting several times before entering the pupal stage. When the adult beetle emerges from the pupa, it is ready to breed.

The length of the beetle life cycle varies from one species to another. In some beetles, such as ladybugs, it takes from five to eight weeks to complete the cycle from egg to adult. Stag beetle eggs hatch after two weeks but the larval stage can last up to five years.

Amazing facts

- A click beetle can jump 12 inches (30 centimeters) into the air.

- In severe winter conditions, it is too cold for most adult insects to survive. Some beetles, such as the tiger beetle, bury their eggs in the soil. There the eggs are insulated from freezing temperatures until the following spring, when the larvae are ready to hatch.

- Female glowworms (Lampyris noctiluca) are wingless. On the underside of the last three segments of the abdomen, they have light-producing organs that they use to attract males flying nearby at night.

▼ Male stag beetles are larger than the females. They use their huge antlerlike mandibles to fight other males during the breeding season.

Dragonflies and Damselflies

Dragonflies and damselflies are large, winged insects found in wetlands all over the world. They have two pairs of large, transparent wings, a pair of compound eyes, a pair of short antennae, and a long, often brightly colored abdomen. The wings can move independently, allowing the insect to speed up, brake, hover, and steer with great accuracy. The large and prominent eyes detect movements easily, so these insects can track and catch their prey while flying.

Incomplete metamorphosis

Female dragonflies lay their eggs in freshwater ponds, lakes, and slow-flowing streams. Some species lay their eggs on or in water plants, while others just scatter them. The eggs hatch into wingless nymphs, which remain in the water throughout their development. This may last from one to five years. Dragonflies breathe using gills.

▶ The damselfly rests with its wings folded. It tends to stay near water.

Classification key

PHYLUM	Arthropoda
SUBPHYLUM	Mandibulata
SUPERCLASS	Hexapoda
CLASS	Insecta
ORDER	**Odonata**
FAMILIES	30
SPECIES	about 5,500

Amazing facts

- The compound eye of a dragonfly has about 30,000 lenses.
- Dragonflies can fly at speeds of 59 to 62 miles per hour (95 to 100 kilometers per hour).

Dragonfly nymphs are carnivores, or meat eaters, like the adults. They hunt their prey under water, feeding on other larvae, tadpoles, and even small fish. The lower lip is elongated and hinged in the middle, with two movable claws at the end. The whole structure is called a mask and is tucked under the head when not in use. When a dragonfly nymph sees suitable prey, it pushes the mask forward and uses its claws to capture the food.

▲ Dragonflies have two pairs of powerful wings. In contrast to the damselfly, the wings are spread out when at rest.

When fully grown, the nymph crawls up the stem of a water plant and out of the water. It molts for the last time and emerges as an adult with wings. The adults live for a few weeks. They are powerful fliers, catching their prey of mosquitoes and other small insects while in flight. Male dragonflies search out the females and mating occurs on land. The male grasps hold of the female and the pair may fly around together after mating. The female may lay her eggs in the tissues of water plants. Or she may fly across the surface of water dipping the tip of her abdomen into the water at intervals and scattering her eggs.

Dragonflies or damselflies?

Adult dragonflies and damselflies look quite similar. The main differences are in the structure of the wings and the abdomen. Damselflies have wings that are alike, but dragonflies have hind wings that are broader than the front wings. Dragonflies are generally bigger than damselflies and have a fatter abdomen. They fly faster than damselflies and may travel several miles from water. Damselflies are more slender and delicate than dragonflies, with slower flight. Damselfly nymphs have external gills at the end of the abdomen. Dragonfly nymphs have gills inside the end of the abdomen.

▲ This close-up of the head of a dragonfly shows the large compound eyes that give good all-around vision and help the insect to track its prey.

Flies

Dipterans, or true flies, form one of the largest orders of insects. They are found all over the world, and they range in size from midges just a fraction of an inch long to horseflies with bodies up to 1 inch (2.5 centimeters) in length. True flies eat liquid and have piercing or sucking mouthparts.

True flies are the only insects with just one pair of wings. The hind wings are reduced to a pair of halteres which help the insect fly straight and level. A few species, such as the parasitic sheep ked, do not have wings. The order is divided into species with long antennae and several segments such as crane flies, mosquitoes, and gnats, and those that have shorter antennae with only two or three segments such as the housefly. All the dipterans have a life cycle that involves complete metamorphosis.

▲ Female mosquitoes have syringe-like mouthparts adapted for piercing the skin of mammals and birds. Males have sucking mouthparts and feed on nectar.

Amazing facts

- Houseflies have taste sensors on their feet to detect suitable sources of food.
- Some of the largest flies in the family Mydeidae are up to 2.4 inches (60 millimeters) long.
- A housefly can reach a speed of about 4 miles (7 kilometers) per hour while flying.

Classification key

PHYLUM	Arthropoda
SUBPHYLUM	Mandibulata
SUPERCLASS	Hexapoda
CLASS	Insecta
ORDER	**Diptera**
FAMILIES	130
SPECIES	122,000

◀ Houseflies have thick bodies, short, bristly antennae, and a pair of large compound eyes. Their wings are transparent and have few veins.

Feeding habits

Depending on the species, flies eat decaying plant and animal remains, nectar and plant sap, or the blood of mammals and birds. Flies that feed on blood have sharp mouthparts that pierce through the skin of their victims. Female mosquitoes have mouthparts that fit together to form a tube that they use to pierce the flesh and suck up blood. Other blood-sucking flies, such as horseflies and stable flies, have similar sharp structures. Houseflies sip liquid food through a fleshy proboscis that has many tiny channels. If houseflies feed on solid food, they may cover it first with saliva containing digestive juices. This helps them turn he food into liquid and then suck it up.

Pests and disease

Blood-sucking flies, such as mosquitoes and tsetse flies, are serious pests. If a blood-sucking fly bites a person infected with malaria, yellow fever, or sleeping sickness, the insect can pass the disease on to the blood of the next person it bites.

In addition, houseflies can contaminate human food. They may feed on manure or garbage and later come into contact with human food. When feeding, houseflies often regurgitate some of their previous meal, and this can spread harmful bacteria and diseases such as typhoid and cholera.

▲ Hoverflies feed on pollen and nectar. They have brightly colored bodies. Many species look like bees or wasps, but they do not sting.

Crustacea

Most crustaceans are aquatic. They range in size from tiny water fleas to large crabs and lobsters. In the larger crustaceans, the exoskeleton is usually hard and thickened with calcium carbonate everywhere except the joints. Within the group there is a great deal of variation in body shape. Usually the body is divided into the head, thorax, and abdomen. However, in many species the head is fused with the thorax to form a cephalothorax. A shieldlike outgrowth from the head called the carapace extends back over the body and protects the gills.

In a typical crustacean, the head has two pairs of antennae, one pair of compound eyes on stalks, and paired mouthparts. The segments of the cephalothorax and the abdomen each bear a pair of limbs. These may be adapted for swimming, crawling, or feeding. There is sometimes a tail portion, called the telson, which is used in swimming. Not all of these features are seen in every class. For example, water fleas have no obvious body segments, and barnacles have a small head and abdomen.

▼ The stalked eyes of this Australian mud crab give an all-around view. The tough exoskeleton and well-developed claws are also typical of this group of crustaceans.

Classification key

PHYLUM	Arthropoda
SUBPHYLUM	Mandibulata
SUPERCLASS	**Crustacea**
CLASSES	6 – Branchiopoda (water fleas and brine shrimp); Ostracoda (oyster shrimp); Maxillopoda (copepods and barnacles); Malacostraca (crabs, lobsters and prawns); Remipedia (eyeless, primitive forms); Cephalocarida (tiny, shrimplike form)
ORDERS	37
FAMILIES	540
SPECIES	more than 40,000

With its long, slender legs and prominent eyes, the spider crab has an appropriate name. Despite its fearsome appearance, this crab feeds on sponges and seaweeds.

Larval forms

Most crustacean eggs hatch into minute larvae, which are very different from the adults. The simplest types of larvae are not segmented, but they have three pairs of appendages, that they use to move about and eat. In some species, like water fleas, these larvae feed, grow, and molt, each time looking more like adults. In other species, such as barnacles and crabs, the larvae are free-swimming and there may be two or more different larval stages. In groups in which the adults are fixed in one place, such as barnacles, or are slow-moving, such as crabs, free-swimming larvae help the species spread to new areas and move to suitable habitats.

Amazing facts

○ The pill wood louse, *Armadillidium vulgare*, can roll itself into a ball to escape predators. Scientists also think that this reduces water loss and prevents the animal from drying up.

○ Water fleas get their name because the movements of their antennae make them appear to be hopping like fleas.

○ Museum workers use wood lice to clean the flesh from delicate vertebrate skeletons.

▶ Wood lice are found in clusters under stones and in damp places. They have seven pairs of walking legs on the thorax and appendages on the abdomen that are used for breathing.

Crabs and Lobsters

Crabs and lobsters belong to a large group of crustaceans called the Malacostraca. They are found all over the world, from the open seas and seashores to freshwater and land habitats. Usually, animals in this group have tough exoskeletons, eyes on stalks, and prominent antennae. There are eight segments in the thorax and six segments in the abdomen. The first pair of walking legs on the thorax usually has large claws, or pincers, at the end for holding and tearing food. At the end of the abdomen there may be a tail fan, or telson, that is used for swimming. The head and thorax together form the cephalothorax and are covered by the carapace. Feathery gills lie under the carapace. On the abdomen, there are often appendages that are used for swimming, mating, or holding the eggs until they hatch.

◄ The large, well-developed pincers of this common lobster are used for holding prey and tearing food.

Crawlers

Crabs and lobsters are crawlers, rather than swimmers. They all have a heavy exoskeleton that prevents them moving from rapidly in water but protects them from predators. The Malacostraca group includes lobsters, crayfish, squat lobsters, and true crabs. The lobsters and crayfish have long antennae, large abdomens, and broad telsons. If frightened, a lobster can bend its abdomen and use its telson to move backward suddenly. Squat lobsters have smaller abdomens and no telsons, but they can still swim backward to escape their enemies. True crabs have much smaller abdomens that are bent forward underneath so that only the flattened carapace is seen. The antennae are short and the pincers are well developed.

Classification key

PHYLUM	Arthropoda
SUBPHYLUM	Mandibulata
SUPERCLASS	Crustacea
CLASS	**Malacostraca**
ORDER	Decapoda
SPECIES	20,000

Spider crabs

Spider crabs are true crabs. Their carapaces are extended to form a spiny projection called the rostrum. Spider crabs have extremely long legs in relation to their bodies. They use their small pincers to cover themselves with seaweed so that they can hide from predators. Spider crabs range in size from the yellowline arrow crab, which grows up to 2.4 inches (6 centimeters) long to the enormous Japanese island crab, whose legs may reach almost 5 feet (1.5 meters) long.

▼ Hermit crabs live in the empty shells of sea snails. Eventually the crabs grow too big for the shell and must move to a new home.

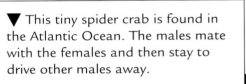

Amazing facts

- About 100 million red crabs live on Christmas Island in the Indian Ocean. Every year they migrate from their homes inland to the coast, where they mate and produce their eggs.
- The robber crab, *Birgus latro*, lives on islands in the Pacific and climbs palm trees to feed on coconuts.

▼ This tiny spider crab is found in the Atlantic Ocean. The males mate with the females and then stay to drive other males away.

Common shore crab

The common shore crab is a typical example of a true crab. It is found in mud flats and sandy regions of the shore, as well as in rock pools in Europe and North America. Like all true crabs, the shore crab has a thick carapace covering the cephalothorax. The abdomen is a flap that is tucked underneath the body. The common shore crab has a pair of pincers with serrated edges that it uses to grab hold of small animals and other food. It has four pairs of walking legs. The fourth pair is adapted for swimming and is more flattened and paddle-like than the other three pairs. On its head the crab has short antennae, compound eyes on stalks, and a pair of strong mandibles, or jaws, that hold food. Other mouthparts shred the food and push it into the mouth.

Amazing facts

- Crab larvae form part of the large number of tiny organisms found in the surface layers of the sea. These organisms form zooplankton, or animal plankton, which is the food of fish such as herrings.
- All the larval stages of crabs have prominent eyes on stalks.
- Male crabs are aggressive and will fight each other for the chance to mate with a female.

▼ This female Christmas Island red crab has a large, dark-colored mass of fertilized eggs attached to her abdomen.

◀ Although the larvae of crabs are adapted for swimming, an adult crab moves slowly in water.

Breeding and life cycle

Mating occurs between male and female crabs just after the female has molted. The female protects the fertilized eggs by carrying them on her abdomen. The eggs are held by special branched appendages on the underside of the abdomen. These appendages have tiny spines, called setae, which help the eggs stay attached. Larvae called zoea hatch out of the eggs. The larvae are tiny and do not look like crabs at all. They have a slender, curved abdomen and a carapace with two long spines on it, one pointing forward and one backward. Each larva swims around, feeds, grows, and molts several times. As it grows, the larva develops limbs on the thorax and on the abdomen and changes into the next larval stage, called the megalopa. In this stage, it looks much more like a crab. It comes to the surface and swims around before molting to become a fully-formed crab. It is at this last molt that the flap of the abdomen folds under the body and is no longer used for swimming.

▲ These crab larvae swim, feed, and grow, molting several times before they develop into adult crabs .

Prawns and Shrimp

True prawns and shrimp belong to the same order as crabs and lobsters (Decapoda) and share many of their characteristics. With their long abdomens, they look more like lobsters than crabs. Prawns and shrimp are swimmers rather than crawlers. They have lighter exoskeletons, and their bodies are flattened from side to side. This allows them to move easily through water. Prawns and shrimp are found all over the world in freshwater and marine habitats.

The decapod prawns and shrimp are transparent or greenish-brown in color. They have muscular abdomens with broad telsons that are used for swimming. There are eight pairs of appendages on the thorax. The first three pairs are mouthparts. The other five pairs of appendages are used for walking. On the abdomen are five pairs of short swimming legs called pleopods.

Amazing facts

- Baleen whales migrate to Antarctic waters to feed on krill. One whale can eat as much as 2.2 tons of krill in one feeding session.

- In schools of krill, there may be up to 40 pounds (18 kilograms) of organisms per cubic yard.

- Krill have light-producing organs on their thoraxes. These give off a greenish light.

Classification key

PHYLUM	Arthropoda
SUBPHYLUM	Mandibulata
SUPERCLASS	Crustacea
CLASS	Malacostraca
ORDERS	Amphipoda (freshwater shrimp)
	Decapoda (true prawns and shrimp)
	Stomatopoda (mantis shrimp)
	Euphausiacea (krill)

▲ Prawns have a well-developed rostrum, distinguishing them from edible shrimp. Both have a pair of long, backward-facing antennae.

Shrimp or prawn?

Prawns and shrimp have a carapace with a beaklike projection at the front called the rostrum. In prawns, the rostrum is long and sometimes has a serrated edge. The rostrum of a shrimp is much smaller and looks like a spine. In many parts of the world, no distinction is made between the two, and the term *shrimp* may be used for both.

▼ The mantis shrimp, which is found in tropical and subtropical seas, catches prey using its second pair of legs. These legs are large. They can spear and crush small animals.

▼ The pistol shrimp has a large claw that it uses to punch holes in the exoskeletons of crustaceans. The noise made by this claw as the pincers close gives the shrimp its name.

Freshwater shrimp, such as those in the genus *Gammarus*, belong to the order Amphipoda. They have bodies that are flattened from side to side. They can be found in freshwater streams and around the stones on seashores. Mantis shrimp belong to the order Stomatopoda and get their name from their resemblance to the praying mantis.

Importance in food chains
Prawn and shrimp larvae form part of the zooplankton in aquatic habitats. The larvae and the adults feed on tiny organisms in the water and are, in turn, eaten by larger organisms. The shrimplike krill, which belong to the family Euphausiidae, are abundant in cooler oceans and are the main food of baleen whales. There are about 85 different species of krill. They range in size from 0.3 to 2.8 inches (8 to 70 millimeters) long and are found on the surface as well as in deeper water. Krill feed on tiny plants called diatoms and are eaten by fish and birds as well as whales.

Copepods and Barnacles

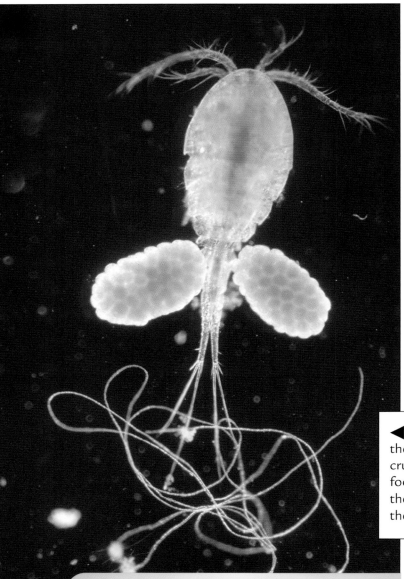

Copepods are tiny aquatic crustaceans found in large numbers in freshwater and marine habitats. They have a cephalothorax but no carapace and no limbs on the abdomen. The adults and larvae form an important part of marine plankton, feeding on tiny plants and then themselves being the prey of larger aquatic organisms such as herrings. Some groups of copepods spend part of their life cycles as parasites attached to other animals, such as fish and whales. Others are free-living and are not parasitic as larvae or as adults.

◀ This freshwater copepod belongs to the genus *Cyclops*. It is a transparent crustacean with mandibles that break its food up into pieces. The females keep the fertilized eggs in a pair of egg sacs on the abdomen.

Amazing facts

- *Cyclops* (a type of copepod with only one eye) get their name from the mythical giants that were said to have a single eye in the middle of the forehead.
- Barnacles were originally thought to be related to mollusks until their larvae were shown to be like those of other crustaceans.

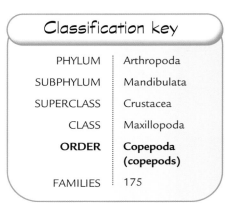

Classification key

PHYLUM	Arthropoda
SUBPHYLUM	Mandibulata
SUPERCLASS	Crustacea
CLASS	Maxillopoda
ORDER	**Copepoda (copepods)**
FAMILIES	175

Barnacles

Barnacles are marine crustaceans. The adults live in groups attached to rocks, wood, ships' bottoms, and the bodies of animals such as turtles and mollusks. Barnacles are found all over the world. The adult body is made up mostly of the thorax, which is surrounded by chalky plates of exoskeleton. The head and the abdomen are very small. They all have feathery thoracic limbs, called cirri, which they use to filter food from the water.

Acorn barnacles (*Balanus balanoides*) are often the most common animals on rocky shores. They are found in large numbers encrusting rocks in the zone between high and low tide. When the animal is not covered by water, the plates of the exoskeleton completely enclose it. When the tide comes in and covers the rocks, the top plates open and six pairs of cirri sweep through the water, filtering out food.

Barnacles are hermaphrodites, which means they have both male and female sex organs. However, the eggs are fertilized by sperm cells from a nearby barnacle. The fertilized eggs stay inside the animal, and the larvae are released only when the conditions for survival are good. There are two types of larvae. The first is an unsegmented, simple larva called a nauplius larva. This grows and molts several times and becomes a cypris larva. The cypris larva does not feed but finds a suitable place to settle. It produces a cementlike substance to anchor itself and then changes into the adult form.

▲ Goose barnacles (*Lepas* species) are bigger than acorn barnacles. They attach themselves to floating timbers and other supports by means of a flexible stalk.

Classification key

PHYLUM	Arthropoda
SUBPHYLUM	Mandibulata
SUPERCLASS	Crustacea
CLASS	Maxillopoda
ORDER	**Cirripedia (barnacles)**
FAMILIES	31
SPECIES	10,000

▶ Acorn barnacles attach themselves to rocks on the shore. Some shores have around 50,000 per square yard.

Minor Classes

There are several minor classes of crustaceans, many of which are of great importance in aquatic food chains. Some feed on dead organic material, others on tiny plants and algae, and a few feed on smaller arthropods.

Remipedia

This small group of crustaceans was not discovered until the 1980s. They are found in the Caribbean and around Australia in deep caves that connect with the sea. The remipedia's body is divided into a head that has antennae but no eyes and a trunk section made up of 32 similar segments. Each segment has a pair of paddle-like appendages used for swimming.

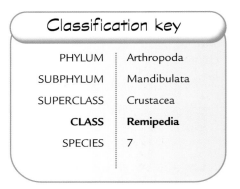

Classification key

PHYLUM	Arthropoda
SUBPHYLUM	Mandibulata
SUPERCLASS	Crustacea
CLASS	**Remipedia**
SPECIES	7

Branchiopoda

Branchiopods are usually found in freshwater, although some species can live in saltwater habitats. Brine shrimp (family Artemiidae) are found all over the world in saltwater lakes and pools. They have flat, leaflike appendages with fine bristles that they wave around to trap food and swim. Water fleas (*Daphnia* genus) also belong to this group. They do not have obvious segments and they move in a series of jerks using their antennae.

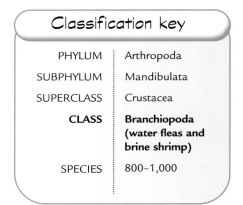

Classification key

PHYLUM	Arthropoda
SUBPHYLUM	Mandibulata
SUPERCLASS	Crustacea
CLASS	**Branchiopoda (water fleas and brine shrimp)**
SPECIES	800–1,000

Amazing facts

- Some mussel shrimp species emit light to attract mates.
- The presence of different fossils in layers of rocks, or rock strata, can help geologists to date the rocks. Ostracod fossils have been used to locate layers of rock that contain oil.

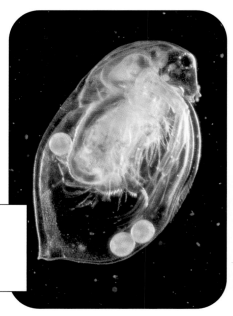

▶ *Daphnia* (a branchiopod) is often found in freshwater plankton. All of its body organs are visible through the transparent carapace. The eggs develop in a pouch attached to the body.

► Fairy shrimp are branchiopods with a long body and no carapace. They use their limbs for feeding as well as locomotion.

Cephalocarida

Cephalocarids live in silt or sand on the seabed and feed on dead organic material. They are found up to depths of 4,950 feet (1500 meters). They have heads, thoraxes made up of eight segments, abdomens of eleven segments, and telsons. The thorax has paddle-like appendages, but there are no appendages on the abdomen. The biggest cephalocarid is about 0.14 inches (3.5 millimeters) long.

Classification key	
PHYLUM	Arthropoda
SUBPHYLUM	Mandibulata
SUPERCLASS	Crustacea
CLASS	**Cephalocarida**
SPECIES	9

Ostracoda

Ostracods are found in marine and freshwater habitats. Most of an ostracod's body consists of a head with five pairs of appendages. Ostracods range from 0.04 to 0.12 in. (1 mm to 3 cm) in length. They are totally enclosed by the carapace and have only the antennae outside their bodies. Most species live at the bottom of seas or lakes. Ostracods crawl around in the mud feeding on decaying matter or other small animals.

Classification key	
PHYLUM	Arthropoda
SUBPHYLUM	Mandibulata
SUPERCLASS	Crustacea
CLASS	**Ostracoda (mussel shrimp)**
FAMILIES	60
SPECIES	6,000

► The body of an ostracod does not have distinct segments and is totally enclosed by its carapace.

Centipedes and Millipedes

Centipedes and millipedes are land-dwelling arthropods with many legs. Both are divided into two parts: a head and a long, slender body called a trunk. The head has one pair of antennae and usually two pairs of biting mouthparts. The eyes, if present, are simple. Typically, there is one pair of legs on each segment of the trunk. The exoskeleton does not have a waxy, waterproof layer, so centipedes and millipedes tend to live in damp habitats, such as soil or leaf litter, so that they do not dry up.

Classification key

PHYLUM	Arthropoda
SUBPHYLUM	Mandibulata
SUPERCLASS	Myriapoda
CLASSES	**2 – Chilopoda (centipedes) and Diplopoda (millipedes)**
ORDERS	16
FAMILIES	144
SPECIES	13,700

Centipedes

Centipedes are found all over the world, from temperate to tropical regions. Their bodies are long and flattened. There are at least sixteen segments making up the trunk, with one pair of legs on each segment. The long, thread-like antennae are the centipede's main sense organs. The appendages on the first trunk segment are adapted to form a pair of poison claws, which are hollow structures connected to poison glands. Centipedes are carnivores. They hunt at night for slugs, earthworms, and soft-bodied insects. They grasp their prey using the claws and inject poison into them.

After mating with a male, the female lays the fertilized eggs in soil. The eggs hatch into miniature adults, but have fewer segments. As the young feed and grow, their bodies grow more segments.

▼ Centipedes have one pair of legs on each segment of the trunk. They can move quickly across the ground.

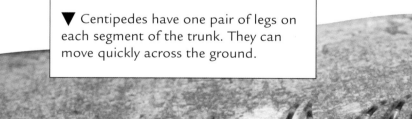

▲ Scolopendrids are brightly colored. This species includes some of the largest centipedes in the world, reaching 10.4 in. (26 cm) in length. This one has caught a tarantula.

Millipedes

Millipedes have more cylindrical-shaped bodies. The number of trunk segments varies from one species to another. Some have 11 segments, while others have more than 100. The trunk segments are fused together in pairs and are called diplosegments. Inside each diplosegment, there are two of everything, so it follows that each has two pairs of legs on the outside. Millipedes are herbivores and feed mainly on decaying plants. However, they will also eat roots and fruits. When threatened, millipedes roll up into a ball and produce a bad-smelling liquid to deter their enemies. After mating, the female lays groups of eggs in a nest that she guards until they hatch.

Amazing facts

- A tropical centipede, *Scolopendra gigantica*, may grow to a length of 10.4 inches (260 millimeters).
- Millipedes vary in size, with the smallest being about 0.08 inches (2 millimeters) long and the biggest up to 11.2 inches (280 millimeters) long.
- The largest millipedes may have up to 750 legs—not a thousand as their name suggests.

▶ Despite having a larger number of legs, millipedes move more slowly than centipedes. The legs appear to move in a wave as the millipede crawls through leaf litter.

Arachnids

Arachnids belong to the subphylum Chelicerata, which also includes sea spiders and horseshoe crabs. All chelicerates have a body divided into two parts: a cephalothorax and an abdomen. There are no antennae, and the first pair of appendages are called chelicerae. These are like pincers or fangs and are used for feeding. The second pair of appendages are the pedipalps. These may be used to capture prey, or they may be covered in tiny hairs that detect changes in temperature, air currents, and movement.

Most arachnids live on land. They are nearly all carnivores that feed on other arthropods such as insects. In addition to the chelicerae and pedipalps, there are four pairs of walking legs on the cephalothorax. Arachnids do not have jaws or antennae. Their food is broken up by the chelicerae. Many arachnids have sensory hairs all over the body.

▼ Many spiders spin intricate webs in which they trap their prey.

Spiders

Spiders form one of the largest arachnid orders. Large numbers of individuals may be present in a habitat. Spiders differ from other arachnids because they have as many as eight eyes, although in a few families there are only two or six eyes. Spiders also have the ability to produce silk, which they use to make webs, trap their prey, and make cocoons. Spiders are all predators that feed on insects.

Ticks and mites

There are more than 30,000 different species of ticks and mites. Most species are very small. Mites are about 0.04 inches (1 millimeters) long while the largest ticks can be up to 1.2 inches (30 millimeters) long. There is no clear division between the cephalothorax and the abdomen. Most mites live in soil and leaf litter, and some species feed on stored food products such as flour and cheese. Ticks are bloodsuckers, and all are parasites. Their soft, flexible abdomens swells up after a meal of blood.

▲ The typically rounded body of this tick shows no division between the cephalothorax and the abdomen.

Classification key

PHYLUM	Arthropoda
SUBPHYLUM	Chelicerata (arachnids, sea spiders, and horseshoe crabs)
CLASS	**Arachnida**
ORDERS	12 (including spiders, scorpions, harvestmen, ticks, and mites)
FAMILIES	450
SPECIES	7,500

▶ The large pedipalps of this imperial scorpion are adapted for catching prey such as spiders and small lizards.

Amazing facts

- There may be as many as 150,000 mites in 1 square yard (1 square meter) of undisturbed grassland.
- After a meal of blood, the abdomen of a female sheep tick may swell to two or three times its normal size.

Scorpions

Scorpions are found in tropical climates. They have elongated bodies, and the segmentation of the abdomen is more obvious than it is in other arachnids. They have large pedipalps with pincers that they use for grabbing their prey. The tail forms a sting and can be used to inject poison into prey .

Using poisons

Scorpions, pseudoscorpions, and most spiders can make poisonous substances called venom. Venom is used to kill prey or to paralyze it so that it cannot escape. Sometimes venom is used to warn off a predator.

Venom is usually made in special glands in the cephalothorax. It is injected into the prey by fangs. In spiders, chelicerae are adapted to form the fangs. In each fang, there is a duct, or passage, down the middle for the venom to pass into the victim. The fangs have a stabbing action, rather than a bite. The mouthparts of spiders are for sucking rather than biting.

Scorpions have venom glands in their tails . The stinger is formed in the telson and has a sharp point. When threatened, or to calm struggling prey, the scorpion arches its abdomen over its head and uses its stinger. Pseudoscorpions look like true scorpions but do not have a stinger or a tail. Their venom glands are in the claws of the pedipalps. As they grasp their prey, venom is injected into its body.

▲ In pseudoscorpions, the venom is made in glands in the pincers of the adapted pedipalps. The inner edge of these pincers is smooth. During courtship, males and females grab hold of each other's pedipalps.

▲ Wolf spiders are found all over the world, even in Arctic regions.

Amazing facts

○ The Brazilian wandering spider (*Phoneutria fera*) has the largest venom gland of any spider. It can be up to 0.4 inches (10 millimeters) long and can hold enough venom to kill 225 mice.

○ The lively Italian tarantella dance got its name because it was believed to flush the venom from the bite of a wolf spider, *Lycosa tarantula*, out of the body. The affected person was supposed to dance until he or she fell down on the ground, sweating and exhausted.

Effects of venom

The venom of most spiders is harmful only to insects because it is too weak to harm larger animals. Only about 30 species, including some of the funnel-web spiders, are dangerous to human beings. In many species, such as the black widow spider, the venom affects the nerves and causes paralysis. Some forms of venom affect the victim's blood, causing the blood vessels to break down.

Arachnids can produce chemical substances other than poisons. For example, the abdominal glands of whip scorpions produce harmful acids that can be squirted at attackers. It is likely that some digestive juices are also injected with the venom. These juices can start the process of breaking down the prey so that it can be taken into the mouth and eaten more easily.

▼ This Goliath bird-eating spider has caught a mouse. These spiders will also eat lizards, frogs, poisonous snakes, and small birds.

Spiders

Spiders form one of the largest groups of arachnids. All spiders are carnivores and many will eat members of their own species. Most spiders produce venom.

▲ This orb web spider of the genus *Argiope* has fangs that work like pincers. It catches large insects in its orb-shaped web.

▲ Wolf spiders have excellent eyesight that enables them to hunt at night for their live prey. Male and female wolf spiders often dance together before mating.

Body shape

A spider's body is clearly divided into two parts—the cephalothorax and the abdomen—with a narrow waist between them. On the head, the chelicerae form the poison fangs and the pedipalps are sensory structures. There are eight simple eyes arranged in two or three rows. Spiders have four pairs of hollow legs attached to the cephalothorax. The abdomen is covered in soft, stretchy skin. At the tip of the abdomen, there is a group of spinnerets, which are structures that silk passes through.

Classification key

PHYLUM	Arthropoda
SUBPHYLUM	Chelicerata
CLASS	Arachnida
ORDER	**Aranae**
FAMILIES	about 100
SPECIES	at least 40,000

▲ The jumping spider has excellent vision. It uses some eyes to detect the presence of its prey. Then it uses the front pair of eyes to judge distance so that it can pounce on the victim.

Silk

All spiders make strong, stretchy silk. This silk is used to make webs for trapping prey, to wrap up prey so that it cannot escape, and to make cocoons to protect developing eggs. Inside the spider's abdomen, there are several silk glands, each one producing a different type of silk. The glands open to the outside through fine tubes in the spinnerets. The silk is produced as a liquid that hardens as the spider pulls it into fine threads through the spinnerets.

Family life

Most spiders live alone and come together only to mate. Male spiders are usually smaller than the females. Males have to make sure that they are not mistaken for prey. The males find the females by their scent. Among the web-spinner species, the male finds the web of a female and attracts her attention by making the threads vibrate. If he makes the right moves, she will mate with him. A few weeks after mating, the female lays her eggs and makes a silk cocoon around them. In some species, the female stays with the eggs, often carrying the cocoon around with her. When the eggs hatch, the young spiders look like miniature adults but are transparent and have no hairs, spines, or claws. They molt several times as they grow. Most baby spiders are independent when they hatch, but the females of some species guard and feed their young.

Amazing facts

- A spider's silk is stronger than a steel wire of the same thickness.
- The tiniest known spider, *Patu digua*, is 0.014 inches (0.37 millimeters) long.
- The leg span of the goliath tarantula is up to 10 inches (25 centimeters) long.

Orb Web Spider

Webs can vary in shape and size. Some spiders, such as money spiders, build webs that look like tiny hammocks. Other spiders, such as tarantulas, construct funnel-shaped webs. Orb-shaped webs are circular and are very efficient at trapping flying insects. About 4,000 spider species spin webs of this type. Most of these belong to the family Araneidae.

Classification key

PHYLUM	Arthropoda
SUBPHYLUM	Chelicerata
CLASS	Arachnida
ORDER	Aranae
FAMILY	**Araneidae**
SPECIES	4,000

Web construction

The first stage is to make a bridge line by carrying a thread of silk between two supports. A slack line is then spun below the bridge line. The spider goes back to the middle of the slack line, fixes a thread and drops down to another support. The thread is pulled taut and a Y shape is formed. The center of the Y becomes the center of the web. More threads are added, radiating out like the spokes of a wheel. The spider moves along the existing threads and trails the new thread behind it. The spider pulls each new thread taut with one of its legs before fixing it to a support. When all the spokes are in place, the spider goes back to the center and puts in a temporary spiral to keep them in place.

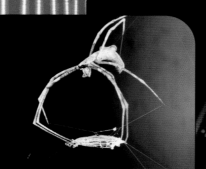

▲ The net-casting spider uses a different method to catch its prey. It hangs upside down, holding the net with four of its legs. When an insect passes, it quickly drops the net over the insect.

So far, all the threads made have been of silk that is not sticky. The spider then moves to an outer edge of the web and begins to lay a final spiral of sticky silk, working inward. At the center, the temporary spiral is eaten as the new spiral is laid. Some spiders leave a nonsticky area in the center of the web and build a platform of silk where they can rest and wait for prey to get stuck.

Catching prey

Other spiders spin a nonsticky signal thread that goes from the center to the edge of the web. When the web is disturbed, the signal thread is moved and alerts the spider. The spider sits at the edge of the web and waits for the signal thread to vibrate. As soon as the spider feels the vibrations, it moves quickly across, keeping to the nonsticky threads. When it reaches its victim, it bites, injecting venom and saliva. It then spins a silk thread to wrap up its meal. Damaged webs can be repaired, or the spider may construct a new web.

▲ This spider traps prey by wrapping it in silk.

Amazing facts

○ A circular web about 10 inches (25 centimeters) across made by a garden spider uses between 66 to 198 inches (20 to 60 meters) of silk.

○ Orb web spiders taken into space built perfect webs despite being weightless.

◄ The sticky, spiral threads of this wheel-shaped orb web make it very difficult for trapped insects to escape.

51

Scorpions

Most scorpions are found in tropical and subtropical regions of the world. Some species have adapted to life in deserts and dry areas, while others live in the humid conditions of tropical rain forests. Scorpions are carnivores, hunting prey at night. They hide in burrows or under stones or logs during the day. Scorpions range in size from 1 to 8 inches (2.5 to 20 centimeters) in length.

Body shape

The body of a scorpion is flattened and divided into a cephalothorax and an elongated abdomen. The upper side of the cephalothorax is protected by the carapace. Scorpions have two pairs of eyes: the central pair can see objects and detect movements, while the eyes on either side can only tell the difference between light and darkness. The pedipalps are large, with pincers adapted for catching prey. The chelicerae also have pincers that are used to tear up food. The bases of the pedipalps and the first two pairs of walking legs are modified for chewing. Most scorpions feed on insects and spiders, but some catch lizards and small mammals.

▼ Scorpions have complicated courtship behavior that ensures that the male is not killed before mating takes place. In many species, males are often killed and eaten by the females after mating.

▲ Female scorpions give birth to live young. They climb onto the mother's back and stay there until their first molt.

Classification key

PHYLUM	Arthropoda
SUBPHYLUM	Chelicerata
CLASS	Arachnida
ORDER	**Scorpiones**
FAMILIES	9
SPECIES	1,400

Amazing facts

- Scorpionids may sting their mates as part of their complex mating ritual.
- Research suggests that scorpions use their chelicerae to kill their victims. They use poison only if their prey resists.

The sting

Inside the telson at the end of the abdomen are large venom glands that produce deadly poison. On the outside, there is a sharp spine that is used to pierce the victim and inject a venom that paralyzes the victim. Some species, such as *Centruroides noxius*, are found in the United States. These scorpions are dangerous to human beings, but will sting only if threatened.

Pseudoscorpions and other look-alikes

Members of several other arachnid orders look like scorpions, but they differ slightly in structure and their ability to sting. Pseudoscorpions are only as big as 0.32 inches (8 millimeters) long. They live in leaf litter, in soil, or under stones. They have venom glands in their large pedipalps, but the abdomen is short and there is no stinger. Wind scorpions have no poison glands at all. Prey is killed by the chelicerae and held down by the pedipalps while it is being eaten. Whip scorpions have long, segmented telsons at the end of their abdomens. They produce an acidic liquid that they can squirt over an attacker to temporarily blind it.

▶ When a scorpion is about to attack, it holds its claws wide apart.

Arthropods Under Threat

Human beings can be harmed by the activities of arthropods. Many species destroy crops or cause serious diseases. On the other hand, people benefit from arthropods. Some provide food and products such as beeswax and honey, others pollinate crops, and others break down animal and plant remains.

Certain arthropod species are under threat of extinction. There are about 50 crustacean species and 49 insect species on the Red List of Threatened Species published by the IUCN, also known as the World Conservation Union. These include some crabs, brine shrimp, butterflies, and beetles.

Habitat change

The disappearance of land habitats such as rain forests and natural grasslands has a major impact on insect and arachnid populations. When plants that provide food for insects are removed, the entire food chain suffers. Scientists think there are thousands of rain forest species, particularly insects and other arthropods, that have yet to be discovered. If the rain forests disappear, these species, together with other organisms, may become extinct before anyone discovers them.

▼ Some butterfly species depend on a narrow range of food plants. Destruction of habitats could result in the loss of these plants and the extinction of the butterflies.

Pollution

Pollution involves the addition of chemicals and other waste into natural ecosystems. These substances can get into the bodies of arthropods, either directly or through eating infected organisms. There is often an increased quantity of these harmful substances in the animals higher up the food chain. If poisonous chemicals get into the bodies of insects, then these chemicals will be passed on to birds or fish that eat large numbers of the insects. This can happen with poisonous chemicals that are sprayed on crops to kill pests. The chemicals used to kill harmful insect pests can kill harmless insects as well.

▲ Slash and burn agriculture, in which trees are cut down and burned to clear the land, destroys habitats such as rain forests. Some arthropod species may become extinct before they have been discovered.

Aquatic ecosystems

When harmful chemicals get into water, many arthropod species with aquatic larvae become affected. In freshwater ecosystems, insect larvae are at risk. In marine ecosystems, pollution can destroy plankton. Oil pollution can have a huge impact on marine habitats because it covers the surface of the ocean with oil and threatens all plant and animal life in the area. Crustaceans such as crabs, lobsters, and prawns are harvested in large numbers and eaten by human beings. They are becoming scarce in some areas.

Amazing facts

- Tropical rain forests are thought to contain more than half of all the known species of animals, including thousands of species of social insects, such as bees, wasps, and ants.
- Studies of the way in which insects fly have contributed to the development of aircraft.

◄ Oil pollution is a serious threat to all marine life.

Protecting Arthropods

More research is needed to find and name all of the species that inhabit different ecosystems. Many arthropods are tiny and therefore escape notice. However, they are of great importance in food chains. The survival of one species is important for the survival of others in the same habitat.

Protecting habitats

A species' natural habitat should provide all its survival needs. By setting up national parks and wildlife reserves, people can preserve many habitats. These parks and reserves do protect larger animals, such as mammals, birds, and reptiles. They also preserve arthropods, which, though not always noticeable, are just as important in keeping a balance in the ecosystem.

▼ The spiders and butterflies shown here were collected from the wild for sale to tourists. Laws now protect some rare species.

▲ The abundance of flowers in gardens and fields provides food for butterflies such as this peacock butterfly.

Many insects, such as butterflies and moths, depend on specific plants to lay their eggs and provide food for their larvae. The reduction in the use of weed killers on roadsides contributes to the growth of more wildflowers. At the same time, the management of woodlands and grasslands encourages the preservation of different habitats. Both measures increase the range of plants and habitats available to insects. This can help control pest organisms because it provides habitats for their predators.

Breeding programs

One way of conserving species is to breed them in captivity so that they can be released back into the wild. Tropical butterflies, such as birdwings, are bred in captivity for collectors. This protects the species and stops them from being collected in the wild. All over the world, breeding programs could be used to boost the numbers of many declining arthropod species in the wild.

Amazing facts

- The world's largest butterflies, the birdwings, are now protected by law. In 1966, a collector paid almost $1,000 for *Troides allotei*, a rare birdwing from the Solomon Islands.

- Wood ants protect forests because they eat harmful insects. In Germany in 1880, the wood ant was the first insect to be protected by conservation law.

Legislation

Laws and agreements can be made between countries to protect wildlife, ban the killing of certain animals, or limit the number that can be caught or killed. There are agreements between countries to protect arthropod species. For example, it is illegal to collect certain rare butterflies and moths.

▲ Stag beetles take a long time to grow to maturity. They spend up to five years as grubs, eight months as pupae, and then live only a few months as adults. Destruction of their woodland habitat could quickly result in their extinction.

Classification

Scientists know of about two million different kinds of animals. With so many species, it is important that they be classified into groups so that they can be described more accurately. The groups show how living organisms are related through evolution and where they belong in the natural world. A scientist identifies an animal by looking at features such as the number of legs or the type of teeth. Animals that share the same characteristics belong to the same species. Scientists place species with similar characteristics in the same genus. The genera are grouped together in families, which in turn are grouped into orders, and orders are grouped into classes. Classes are grouped together in phyla and finally, phyla are grouped into kingdoms. Kingdoms are the largest groups. There are five kingdoms: monerans (bacteria), protists (single-celled organisms), fungi, plants, and animals.

Naming an animal

Each species has a unique Latin name that consists of two words. The first word is the name of the genus to which the organism belongs. The second is the name of its species. For example, the Latin name of the Peacock butterfly is *Nymphalis io* and that of the Camberwell beauty is *Nymphalis antiopa*. This tells us that these animals are grouped in the same genus but are different species. Many animals are given common names that vary from one part of the world to another. For example, the common shiny wood louse, *Oniscus asellus*, is also called a "bibble bug," a "gammer sow," a "coffin cutter," a "pill bug," or a "cudworm."

▼ Praying mantids belong to the order Mantodea. They have triangular heads and large eyes and are the only insects able to turn their heads and look behind them.

Sometimes there are very small differences between individuals of the same species. So there is an extra division called a subspecies. To show that an animal belongs to a subspecies, another name is added to the end of the Latin name. For example, there are several subspecies of migratory locust, *Locusta migratoria*: *L. migratoria manilensis* (Oriental), *L. migratoria migratoria* (Asian), and *L. migratoroides* (African).

This table shows how a housefly is classified.

Classification	Example: housefly	Features
Kingdom	Animalia	Houseflies belong to the animal kingdom because they have many cells, need to eat food, and are formed from a fertilized egg.
Phylum	Arthropoda	A housefly is an arthropod because it has a segmented body, an exoskeleton, and jointed legs.
Subphylum	Mandibulata	Animals that possess chewing mouthparts and antennae belong to the subphylum Mandibulata.
Superclass	Hexapoda	Hexapods have three pairs of legs.
Class	Insecta	Houseflies are insects because they have a thorax with three pairs of legs, one or two pairs of wings, and an abdomen.
Order	Diptera	Dipterans have a pair of front wings and a pair of halteres for balancing.
Family	Muscidae	Members of this family are drab colored with hairy bodies and mouthparts adapted for sucking up liquids.
Genus	*Musca*	A genus is a group of species that are are more closely related to one another than to any other group in the family. *Musca* is the genus for the housefly.
Species	*M. domestica*	A species is a group of individuals that can interbreed successfully. *M. domestica* is the complete name for the housefly.

Arthropod Evolution

The exact origins of the arthropods are still unknown, but scientists assume that they evolved from wormlike animals called annelids. Both groups share some common characteristics, such as the presence of segmented bodies. However, arthropods developed a firm exoskeleton.

▲ In addition to their keen eyesight, which enables them to judge distances, jumping spiders have sturdy front legs that can hold prey firmly when they land on their victims.

Peripatus: the missing link?

In the search for a definite link between annelids and arthropods, scientists investigated the characteristics of a primitive arthropod called Peripatus (the velvet worm). Peripatus has a segmented, wormlike body covered in dry skin, about 20 pairs of short legs, and a head with antennae and mandibles. It looks like a relative of a modern centipede. Fossils of an animal very similar to Peripatus had been discovered in rocks dating back to a time before the evolution of centipedes, more than 500 million years ago. However, more recent fossil evidence, together with details of the life cycle and structure of Peripatus, showed that the ancestors of the velvet worm had no direct links with annelids.

Fossil evidence

There is some evidence to suggest that fossil trilobites were the ancestors of arthropods. Trilobites, known to exist 570 million years ago, have features in common with arthropods—particularly crustaceans. The bodies of trilobites were divided into three parts, they had antennae and jointed limbs, and they had larval stages similar to those of crustaceans.

◀ Tarantulas are mygalomorph spiders, which means their fangs strike downward instead of closing sideways like pincers. They are considered to have evolved before other groups of spiders.

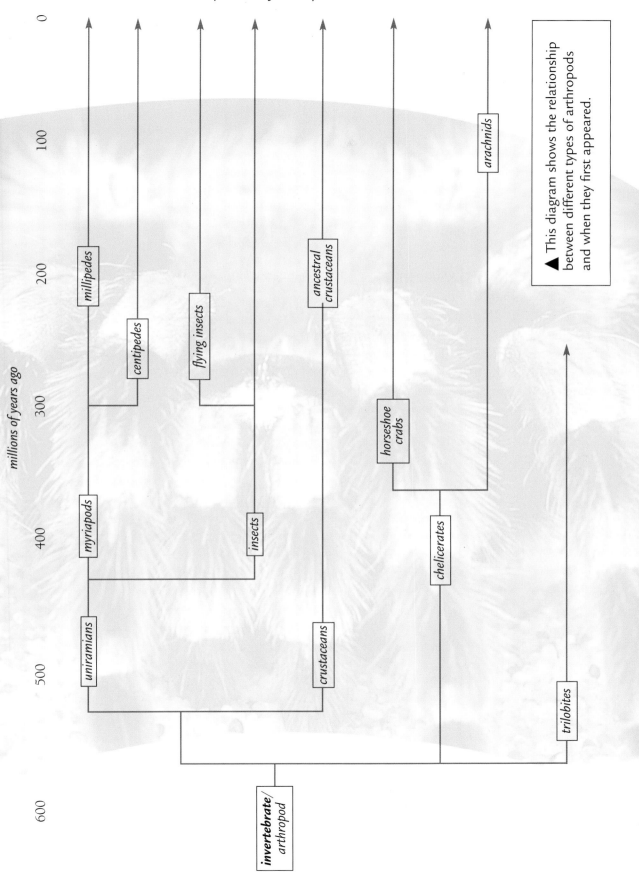

present-day arthropods

millions of years ago

0
100
200
300
400
500
600

millipedes

centipedes

flying insects

ancestral crustaceans

arachnids

myriapods

insects

horseshoe crabs

uniramians

crustaceans

chelicerates

trilobites

invertebrate/ arthropod

▲ This diagram shows the relationship between different types of arthropods and when they first appeared.

Glossary

abdomen rear part of an arthropod's body behind the thorax

adapt change in order to cope with the environment

air current movement of air

antenna (plural: **antennae**) feeler on an arthropod's head that is used to smell, touch, and taste

appendage projection, such as a leg, from the body

aquatic living in water

breed mate and produce young

camouflage coloring that blends with the background, making an animal difficult to see

carapace covering over the cephalothorax in crustaceans and arachnids

carnivore animal that eats other animals

caste group of insects that carries out a particular role in a colony

cephalothorax front part of the body of some arthropods, formed by the head and thorax

characteristic feature or quality of an animal, such as having wings or antennae

chelicera (plural: **chelicerae**) first pair of appendages in an arachnid

chrysalis pupal stage in the life cycle of a butterfly or moth

cocoon case made to contain eggs for spiders, or a pupal case for insects

colony group of organisms, such as bees, that live together

compound eye arthropod eye made up of a large number of tiny lenses

crustacean arthropod that has antennae, eyes on stalks, and a shieldlike covering over the head and thorax

cuticle tough substance that forms the exoskeleton of an arthropod

ecosystem interaction between living organisms and the environment in which they live

evolution organism's slow process of change that makes it better suited to live in its environment

evolve change very slowly over a long period of time

exoskeleton skeleton made of a tough material on the outside of an animal's body

extinct no longer in existence; having permanently disappeared

fertilize coming together of an egg from a female and sperm from a male to form a new individual

food chain grouping of organisms that depend on each other for food

fossil remains, trace, or impression of ancient life preserved in rock

gill part of the body that an aquatic animal uses to collect oxygen from water in order to breathe

haltere modified hind wing of a fly, used as a balancing organ

herbivore animal that eats plants

hermaphrodite organism that has both male and female sex organs

interbreed mate with another animal of the same species

invertebrate animal without a backbone

larva (plural: **larvae**) young animal that looks different from its adult parent and changes shape as it develops; second stage of arthropod life cycle

locomotion movement from one place to another

mandible jaw of an arthropod, especially insects

mate (noun) reproduction partner of the opposite sex

mate (verb) fertilize the eggs

membrane thin sheet of body tissue

metamorphosis insect's change in body shape from larva to adult

migrate travel to a different area for part of the life cycle

molt shed the exoskeleton to allow for growth

nectar sweet liquid produced by plants on which butterflies and bees feed

nymph larva of an insect that undergoes incomplete metamorphosis

organic material from plants or animals

organism any living thing

parasite animal that lives on or in another animal and causes it harm

pedipalp one of the second pair of appendages on an arachnid

plankton group of tiny plants and animals that live in water

pore tiny opening in the surface of skin

predator animal that hunts other animals

prey animal that is killed and eaten by a predator

primitive at an early stage of evolution or development. For example, scorpions are considered to be more primitive than spiders.

proboscis long, thin structure used by butterflies and moths to sip nectar

pupa third stage in the life cycle of an insect that goes through complete metamorphosis

regurgitate bring food back into the mouth

respiration breathing in of oxygen and the breathing out of carbon dioxide

rostrum in insects, set of mouthparts that look like a beak; in crustaceans, the front part of the carapace

serrated looking like a saw

skeleton framework of rigid material giving support to the body either inside or outside

simple eye eye with a single lens

species group of individuals that share many characteristics and which can interbreed to produce offspring

spinneret organ on the abdomen of a spider through which silk is drawn

spiracle opening in the exoskeleton of the thorax and abdomen that allows an insect to breathe

sterile unable to produce offspring

telson tail fan at the end of the abdomen of a crustacean

temperate mild climate

thorax middle part of the body of an arthropod

trachea (plural: **tracheae**) tube that takes air into an animal's body

tropical relating to the hot regions of the world between the tropic of Cancer and the tropic of Capricorn

venom poison

vertebrate animal that has a backbone

zooplankton group of tiny animals that form part of the plankton

Further Information

Fullick, Ann. *Ecosystems & Environment*. Chicago: Heinemann Library, 2000.

Greenaway, Theresa. *Spiders*. Chicago: Raintree, 2004.

Parker, Edward. *Insects and Spiders*. Chicago: Raintree, 2003.

Penny, Malcolm. *Beetles*. Chicago: Raintree, 2004.

Preston-Mafham, Ken. *Butterflies and Moths*. Chicago: Raintree, 2002.

Sachidhanandam, Uma. *Threatened Habitats*. Chicago: Raintree, 2004.

Solway, Andrew. *Classifying Insects*. Chicago: Heinemann Library, 2003.

Townsend, John. *Incredible Arachnids*. Chicago: Raintree, 2005.

Woodward, John. *Flies*. Chicago: Raintree, 2004.

Index

adaptation 6, 7, 12, 15, 18, 24, 28, 30, 34, 35, 42, 45, 46, 52, 59
antennae 4, 8, 9, 14, 23, 26, 28, 30, 31, 32, 34, 36, 40, 41, 42, 44, 59, 60
ants 4, 18–19, 57
appendages 4, 6, 7, 8, 31, 32, 35, 36, 40, 41, 42, 44
arachnids 4, 44–53,61
  body parts 44
  feeding 44, 45, 46, 47, 48, 49, 51, 52, 53

barnacles 30, 31, 38–39
bees 18–19
beetles 7, 10, 12, 13, 22, 24–25, 54, 57
branchiopods 40, 41
breathing (respiration) 7, 9, 26, 31
breeding 10, 11, 17, 25, 35
  see also mating
bugs 22–23
butterflies 9, 11, 12, 13, 14–17, 54, 56, 57, 58
  monarch butterflies 16–17

carapace 30, 32, 33, 34, 35, 36, 38, 40, 41, 52
centipedes 4, 42–43, 60, 61
cephalocarids 41
chelicerae 44, 46, 48, 52, 53
chrysalises 10, 11, 16
cicadas 11, 22, 23
claws 5, 27, 30, 32, 37, 42
cocoons 10, 15, 44, 49
colonies 4, 17, 19, 20, 21
conservation 54–57
copepods 38
crabs 4, 5, 7, 30, 31, 32–35, 54
  common shore crabs 34–35
  spider crabs 31, 33
crustaceans 4, 7, 30–41, 54, 55, 60, 61
  body parts 30
  feeding 31, 32, 33, 34, 37, 39, 40, 41
cuticle 6, 7, 8, 12, 24

damselflies 26–27
defense 15, 16, 24, 31, 32, 33, 43, 46
dragonflies 11, 12, 13, 26–27

eggs
  of arachnids 49
  of centipedes 42
  of crustaceans 31, 32, 34, 35, 38, 39, 40
  of insects 10, 11, 15, 16, 19, 20, 21, 22, 25, 26, 27, 59
evolution 8, 58, 60
exoskeleton 6, 7, 8, 12, 30, 32, 36, 39, 42, 59, 60
extinction 54, 55, 57
eyes 5, 6, 8, 9, 21, 26, 27, 28, 30, 32, 34, 42, 44, 48, 49, 52, 60
  see also sense organs

fighting 24, 25, 34
flies 12, 13, 28–29, 59
food chains 40, 54, 55, 56

habitat loss 54, 55
hexapods 4, 9, 59
horseshoe crabs 4, 44, 61

insects 4, 7, 8–29, 54, 55, 59, 61
  body parts 8
  feeding 14, 15, 16, 17, 18, 19, 27, 28, 29
  flight 12–13, 55
  life cycles 10–11

krill 36, 37

ladybugs 11, 12, 24, 25
larvae
  of crustaceans 31, 34, 35, 37, 38, 39
  of insects 7, 10, 11, 14, 16, 18, 19, 25
lobsters 4, 7, 30, 32–33
locusts 10, 13, 58

mandibles 4, 14, 24, 25, 34, 38, 60
  see also mouthparts
mating 15, 16, 17, 19, 21, 27, 32, 33, 34, 35, 40, 42, 43, 49, 52, 53
  see also breeding
metamorphosis 10, 14, 21, 22, 25, 26, 28
migration 17, 33
millipedes 4, 42–43, 61
mites 4, 45
molting 7, 10, 11, 16, 21, 25, 27, 31, 35, 39, 49, 53
moths 10, 13, 14–15, 56, 57

mouthparts 4, 6, 7, 9, 14, 18, 22, 23, 28, 29, 30, 34, 36, 42, 59
  see also mandibles
myriapods 4, 8, 61

nymphs 10, 11, 21, 22, 26–27

ostracods 40, 41

parasites 18, 28, 38, 45
pedipalps 6, 44, 45, 46, 48, 52, 53
pests 29, 54, 55, 57
pincers 4, 32, 33, 34, 44, 45, 46, 52
plankton 34, 37, 38, 40, 55
pollination 18, 54
pollution 55
prawns 36–37
proboscis 14, 15, 29
pseudoscorpions 46, 53
pupae 10, 11, 15, 16, 19, 25, 57

remipedia 40
rostrum 23, 24, 33, 36

scorpions 6, 45, 46, 47, 52–53
sense organs 4, 6, 7, 8, 9, 28, 42, 44, 48 see also eyes
shrimp 36–37, 40, 41, 54
skippers 15
spiders 4, 5, 7, 44, 46, 47, 48–51, 60
  orb web spider 50–51
  tarantulas 5, 7, 49, 50, 60
spinnerets 48, 49
stag beetles 25, 57
stingers 18, 19, 45, 46, 53

telson 30, 32, 36, 41, 46, 53
termites 20–21
ticks 4, 45

venom 19, 46–47, 48, 51, 53

wasps 18–19
water fleas 4, 30, 31, 40
webs 44, 48, 49, 50–51
wings 8, 9, 10, 11, 12–13, 14, 18, 21, 22, 23, 24, 26, 27, 28, 59
wood lice 31, 58